LANDMARKS OF DEMOCRACY
AMERICAN INSTITUTIONS

THE U.S. CAPITOL

THE HISTORY OF U.S. CONGRESS

STEPHANE HILLARD

PowerKiDS press.

New York

Published in 2018 by The Rosen Publishing Group, Inc.
29 East 21st Street, New York, NY 10010

First Edition

Editor: Elizabeth Krajnik
Book Design: Reann Nye

Photo Credits: Cover Vlad G/Shutterstock.com; p. 5 MPI/Archive Photos/ Getty Images; p. 6 JohnKwan/Shutterstock.com; p. 7 https://commons.wikimedia. org/wiki/File:United_States_Declaration_of_Independence.jpg; p. 8 https:// commons.wikimedia.org/wiki/File:Scene_at_the_Signing_of_the_Constitution_of_ the_United_States.jpg; p. 9 Steve Heap/Shutterstock.com; p. 10 (Capitol Building) J Main/Shutterstock.com; p. 10 (White House) Andrea Izzotti/Shutterstock.com; p. 10 (Supreme Court Building) Steven Frame/Shutterstock.com; p. 11 (Elizabeth Cady Stanton) https://commons.wikimedia.org/wiki/File:Elizabeth_ Stanton.jpg; p. 11 (Jeannette Rankin) https://commons.wikimedia.org/wiki/File: Jeannette_Rankin_cph.3b13863.jpg; p. 12 https://commons.wikimedia.org/ wiki/File:Tom_Cotton_official_Senate_photo.jpg; p. 13 Trevor Collens/ Shutterstock.com; p. 15 Pictorial Parade/Archive Photos/Getty Images; p. 16 Brendan Hoffman/Getty Images News/Getty Images; p. 17 Bill Clark/ CQ-Roll Call Group/Getty Images; p. 18 Chip Somodevilla/Getty Images News/ Getty Images; p. 19 https://commons.wikimedia.org/wiki/File:Paul_Ryan_ official_Speaker_portrait.jpg; p. 20 AFP/Getty Images; p. 21 Mark Wilson/ Getty Images News/Getty Images; p. 22 Ferhat/Shutterstock.com.

Cataloging-in-Publication Data

Names: Hillard, Stephane.
Title: The U.S. Capitol / Stephane Hillard.
Description: New York : PowerKids Press, 2018. | Series: Landmarks of democracy: American institutions | Includes index.
Identifiers: ISBN 9781508160977 (pbk.) | ISBN 9781508160991 (library bound) | ISBN 9781508160984 (6 pack)
Subjects: LCSH: United States Capitol (Washington, D.C.)–Juvenile literature. | Washington (D.C.)–Buildings, structures, etc.–Juvenile literature.
Classification: LCC F204.C2 H55 2018 | DDC 975.3–dc23

Manufactured in the United States of America

CPSIA Compliance Information: Batch #BS17PK: For Further Information contact Rosen Publishing, New York, New York at 1-800-237-9932

CONTENTS

THE FIRST CONTINENTAL CONGRESS

Just like the United States of America, the U.S. Congress didn't always exist. Before the American **Revolution** began in 1775, a group of white male colonists met in secret to make decisions for the other colonists.

This meeting was known as the First Continental Congress. It was held in Philadelphia, Pennsylvania, starting on September 5, 1774. There were 56 people present, **representing** all of the colonies except Georgia. Peyton Randolph from Virginia was elected president of the Congress.

INSTITUTION INSIGHT

The First Continental Congress responded to the Intolerable Acts. These were a set of four punishments British Parliament placed on the American colonists in 1774. Many colonists opposed Britain's authority, and the Intolerable Acts were an attempt to regain Britain's control in the colonies.

Some of the personal rights that the representatives wanted to protect were the ability to own property and to receive fair trials.

The goal of the First Continental Congress was not independence from Britain. Instead, the representatives wanted to ensure that the colonists' personal rights were protected.

5

WAR BREAKS OUT

Disagreements between the colonists and the British resulted in fighting. This fighting turned into full-on battles. Battles at Lexington and Concord in Massachusetts marked the beginning of the American Revolution on April 19, 1775. The British army wanted to catch two of the revolution's leaders and destroy the colonists' weapons. The Americans were able to beat the British at Concord and force them to go back to Boston, Massachusetts.

INSTITUTION INSIGHT

The goals of the Continental Congress were very similar to the goals of the modern Congress. Members of the Continental Congress spoke for the British colonists and, later, the people of the new United States. Today, members of the U.S. Congress speak for the American people they represent. This group of people is supposed to make decisions that are in the people's best interests.

The representatives from 12 colonies voted on July 4, 1776, to adopt the Declaration of Independence. With this, they announced their independence from Great Britain. The New York representatives chose not to vote.

The Second Continental Congress met starting in May 1775. The delegates discussed many topics. Representatives created the Continental army and tried to settle issues with Great Britain. In time, their aim changed to winning full independence.

CONGRESS IS CREATED

After the American Revolution had ended and America had claimed its independence from Britain, it was time to create a set of laws for the new nation. The first **constitution** in the United States was the Articles of Confederation. The Articles of Confederation were in effect from 1781 to 1789. The congress that served during this time was called the Congress of the Confederation.

In 1787, delegates from the 13 states met to make changes to the Articles of Confederation and write the U.S. Constitution. This meeting was called the Constitutional Convention. Altogether, 39 delegates signed the Constitution.

📍 **INSTITUTION INSIGHT**

The Capitol is the building in Washington, D.C., where members of both houses of Congress meet. President George Washington laid the building's first stone on September 18, 1793. Since then, the building has been improved and modernized.

In 1789, a new U.S. Constitution, which is still in effect, was put in place. Article I of the Constitution established Congress, which is made up of the House of Representatives and the Senate.

CONGRESS'S DUTIES

The Constitution assigns duties to each branch of government. Congress is the legislative branch, or the part of the U.S. government that can create and put laws into place. Congress is the only branch of government that can **declare** war. It has the power to accept or refuse the president's choices for **cabinet** members and some other officials. Congress can also conduct **investigations** and has a number of other powers.

The three branches of the U.S. government share equal power. Each branch has its own duties, but all three work together to make the government run smoothly.

JUDICIAL BRANCH

LEGISLATIVE BRANCH

EXECUTIVE BRANCH

⦿ INSTITUTION INSIGHT

In 1866, Elizabeth Cady Stanton became the first woman to run for the House of Representatives. At this time, women weren't able to vote. In 1916, Jeannette Rankin of Montana became the first woman elected to the House of Representatives. In 1920, all U.S. women won the right to vote.

ELIZABETH CADY STANTON   **JEANNETTE RANKIN**

However, the executive branch, or the president and his cabinet, and the judicial branch, or the judges of the Supreme Court, can overturn Congress's choices. Congress can overturn the other two branches' choices, too. This is called a system of checks and balances. It makes sure one branch of the government doesn't get too powerful.

BECOMING A SENATOR

The Senate consists of 100 members called senators. Each of the 50 states has two senators that travel to Washington, D.C., to represent their state. Senators serve six-year terms and can be reelected.

However, not all people can be senators. There are special requirements. The Constitution states that to be a senator, a person must be at least 30 years old. They must have been a citizen for at least nine years and they must live in the state they represent.

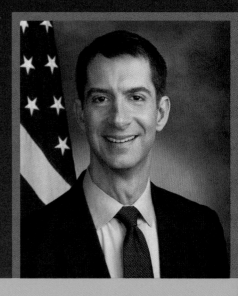

Tom Cotton of Arkansas was the youngest senator of the 114th United States Congress. He was 37 years old when he took office on January 3, 2015.

Bernie Sanders was elected as one of Vermont's senators in 2006. He was reelected in 2012. Before becoming a senator, Sanders served as Vermont's only congressman and the mayor of Burlington, Vermont. He ran for president in 2016.

Aside from these requirements, any American citizen from any background can be elected as a senator.

STRUCTURE OF THE SENATE

To divide Congress's powers, the Constitution created two separate **chambers**. Each chamber meets in a separate room in the Capitol. The Senate is known as the upper chamber of Congress. At first, state legislators elected their state's senators. However, since the 17th Amendment was **ratified** in 1913, people in each state have voted for their senators directly.

The Senate has leaders that help **congressional sessions** run smoothly. The vice president of the United States serves as the president of the Senate. The president pro tempore acts as the Senate president if the vice president is away. *Pro tempore* means "for the time being" in Latin.

The Senate ratifies **treaties**, approves presidential appointments, and votes on **impeachment** charges.

SENATE SESSION, 1955

BECOMING A REPRESENTATIVE

The House of Representatives is made up of 435 representatives. Each state's number of representatives reflects the state's population. This means that some states have more representatives than others. Representatives serve two-year terms and can be reelected.

In the House, there are six non-voting members who represent Washington, D.C., the Virgin Islands, Guam, American Samoa, the Commonwealth of the Northern Mariana Islands, and Puerto Rico. These people can only vote when they are part of a House committee.

LISA BLUNT ROCHESTER
DELAWARE'S REPRESENTITIVE

Just like with senators, there are certain requirements to be a representative. Representatives must be at least 25 years old. They must have been a citizen for at least seven years. Representatives must live in the state they represent, but they aren't required to live in the district they represent.

STRUCTURE OF THE HOUSE OF REPRESENTATIVES

The House of Representatives is known as the lower chamber of Congress. The writers of the Constitution wanted the House to pertain more to the people than the Senate did. From the beginning, the general public could vote for representatives.

The leader of this chamber is the Speaker of the House, who is elected by other representatives. The majority party and **minority** party elect their own leaders. These parties meet separately to discuss matters they are concerned about.

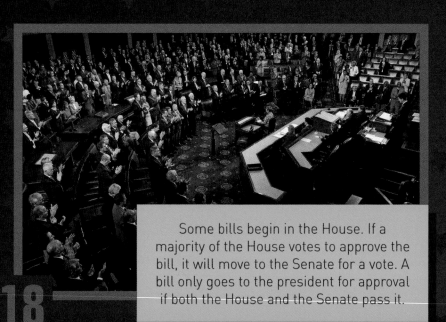

Some bills begin in the House. If a majority of the House votes to approve the bill, it will move to the Senate for a vote. A bill only goes to the president for approval if both the House and the Senate pass it.

The Speaker of the House is third in line for the presidency. This means that, should anything happen to the president, the vice president becomes the president. Then, if anything should happen to the former vice president, the Speaker of the House becomes the president.

PAUL RYAN
54th SPEAKER OF THE HOUSE

The House also has officers who are either elected or appointed. These people are given special tasks that help the House deal with legislation in an organized way.

THE TWO CHAMBERS MEET

Most of Congress's duties are carried out in the individual chambers. However, on some occasions the two chambers must meet together. The Senate and the House come together for a joint session to count the **electoral votes** during an election year.

Congress sometimes holds joint meetings when important people would like to address both chambers. In 2015, Pope Francis addressed a joint meeting of Congress. The pope asked Congress to remember key figures in American history—such as Abraham Lincoln and Martin Luther King Jr.—and reflect on their many successes. These people positively changed the United States.

MARTIN LUTHER KING JR.

The Speaker of the House usually leads joint sessions and joint meetings. However, the Constitution requires that the president of the Senate lead joint sessions when electoral votes are counted.

When he addressed Congress, Pope Francis asked the members to consider the future of young Americans. He said, "It is my desire that this spirit continue to develop and grow, so that as many young people as possible can **inherit** and dwell in a land which has inspired so many people to dream."

PROTECTING THE COUNTRY

Since 1789, the U.S. Congress has been making decisions for all American citizens. Congress creates bills that may become laws, makes sure that cabinet members appointed by the president fit their positions, and provides checks and balances for the executive and judicial branches.

The legislative branch is an important part of the United States government. Because of Congress, new bills are carefully considered and voted on before they can become laws. Thanks to this hard-working group of men and women, citizens' voices are heard and their rights are championed in the halls of the Capitol.

GLOSSARY

cabinet: A group of people who give advice to the leader of a government.

chamber: A legislative or judicial body, especially either of the houses of a two-part legislature.

congressional session: A series of meetings held each year by Congress, or a meeting of one or both houses of Congress.

constitution: The basic laws by which a country, state, or group is governed.

declare: To say or state something in an official or public way.

electoral vote: Votes for the president and vice president of the United States cast by members of the Electoral College. These members are elected by and represent a group of American citizens.

impeachment: A charge made against the holder of a public office for committing a crime while in office.

inherit: To receive something from someone when that person dies.

investigation: The action or process of observing or studying something closely.

minority: A group or party that is a smaller part of a large group.

ratify: To formally approve.

represent: To act or speak officially for someone or something.

revolution: An attempt by many people to end the rule of one government and start a new one.

treaty: An official agreement between two or more countries or groups.

INDEX

WEBSITES

Due to the changing nature of Internet links, PowerKids Press has developed an online list of websites related to the subject of this book. This site is updated regularly. Please use this link to access the list: www.powerkidslinks.com/lod/congress

24